D0878493

salmonpoetry

*Celebrating 35 Years
of Literary Publishing*

In a Changing Light

Phil Lynch

Published in 2016 by
Salmon Poetry
Cliffs of Moher, County Clare, Ireland
Website: www.salmonpoetry.com
Email: info@salmonpoetry.com

ISBN 978-1-910669-45-7

COVER PHOTOGRAPH: *Donal Norton*
COVER DESIGN & TYPESETTING: *Siobhán Hutson*
Printed in Ireland by Sprint Print

Salmon Poetry gratefully acknowledges the support of
The Arts Council / An Chomhairle Ealaoín

For Mary, Eimear and Caroline
and in memory of my parents

Contents

In a
Changing
Light

Against the Wind

I sit on a mountain
the wind tears at my hair
and my clothes
but I sit there;
now and then
I walk against the wind.

Footprints

My thoughts are chirping birds
but all the wings are broken.
The will cannot find the way
the child is now a man
and all the glory fades.

All I ask
is for the storm long since started
to be ended
for this restless soul
to strike a steady beat.

I want to skim across calm waters
to reach the safer shore
from where I can look back
in impish celebration
like the child
who jumped across the stream
and looked behind
at the footprints
he had left.

Changing Light

It was nearly dark
when he came in from the fields
tired from the toils of the day
ready to complain
about the Tilley lamp still unlit,
would he have to light it himself
he asked of no one in particular.
In the shadow of an empty space
beneath the stairs
I stood primed.

The men with the metal boots,
their belts heavy as a gunslinger's,
had spent what seemed like years
digging holes to plant the creosote forest
that stretched across the countryside,
with giant spools of wire unfurled
along roads and lanes and fields.
I marvelled at how they scaled
the heights of those black poles
and worked at right angles to the ground
without falling,
stuntmen all.

In the countdown to dusk I waited
finger on the switch
as if to take its pulse
or like some general in the Kremlin
with his thumb on the red button
waiting for the order to push.
The pre-determined signal came
from my mother at the table
and with all the strength
in my bony digit
I flicked the magic switch.

Outside, the dusk turned instantly to dark.
Inside, the light would never be the same.

Disconnected

They are out of reach now,
the hands that held and clasped,
felt their way through touch and grip,
gone in a confusion of waves
beyond the bottom of the sky.

No tap of fingertips
on far-off keys,
no image flashed on screen
from distant lenses
can bridge the gap,
can match the perfect imperfections
of the touch, the feel, the grasp
of hands we can no longer hold.

Top of the Rock

Standing on top of this mid-Manhattan vantage point,
high as I have ever been,
picking out the green of Central Park
and other landmarks passed in previous days,
gulping in the sights I'd read about in books
or marvelled at on screens,
believing now that they are real
for I have touched their inner flesh.

A passing plane jolts me
back to another rock
on top of which I climbed
so long ago it seems another life;
first time away from home
a child in a lonesome place.

On clearer Winter days
I'd trace the thin white streams
from planes that skimmed
across the Connemara sky
and in the distance
imagine them above my place of birth,
picture there my parents in the yard
or standing in a nearby field looking up
thinking of me.
I'd strain my eyes into a teary blur
then struggle from my craggy perch
back down to bleak and barren earth.

Descending to the Plaza far below
you ask me for my thoughts;
I observe the skaters floating
in the glow of Christmas lights
I say I'm happy to feel so alive
then tell you I've been thinking
that rocks make great foundations.

History Lesson

He strode about the room dictating notes
small in stature, big in voice, full of quotes
he rattled off accounts of family feuds
and wars that lasted a hundred years or more;
his students struggled to keep up with his frantic pace
inventing shorthand to record in hardback copybooks
the dates and places of the battles won and lost.

The wars of old were what they were, history.
The real war was here and now in this theatre
of chalk dust and blackboards, the menace of the man
pitted against the wits of frightened kids. No contest.
He had all the armoury at his disposal
firing off questions like crack snatch squads
between desks to capture hapless prisoners
for interrogation, cross-examination and torture.
The condemned, forced to choose their own punishments
from a menu of techniques
practiced and perfected over decades,
had no escape and no one to tell
about this hidden hell.

But it was a lesson well learned
and one that taught the victory of survival.

Progress

(First broadcast on Irish radio circa 1970)

The main course is finished
the family proceeds to the orchard.
For dessert they eat
the ripening fruit from the trees.
Beneath them the 2pm train streaks through.
Father rushes to his private plane
shouting *I'm late*.
Over the TV controls he calls
I won't be home for tea dear.
He is flying to Peking
for an important meeting
with the Lunar Ambassador
to discuss business prospects.

The 6pm flight from Cape Mao
(formerly named Cape Kennedy)
is delayed because of a dust storm
in Moon-Sey-Ho.
Due to the extended strike by computers
concern continues to grow in New York
as to the amount of food left in their
"Storeroom I"
a quiet place
once called the British Isles
but uninhabited since the afternoon
of the last war.

Latest reports say
the minor famine in Europe
is easing —
only two million have died since noon.
Meanwhile the building up of the planets proceeds,
the plan being
to inhabit the latter

and to re-cultivate the entire earth.
This may be somewhat delayed
by the forthcoming war
expected to decrease the population by half.

Nevertheless,
the great universal progress
continues.

Aftermath

Gentle river of clear water sweet
singing songs as it runs to meet
the sea
torrent of death flowing over the banks
as nature retreats commanding her ranks
to flee.

River of blood flooding the streets where we walk
leaving a trail of distress while our leaders talk
of peace
the old and the young in the shade of a cloud lie praying
when the able slaughter each other, the slaying
may cease.

You sat in a park, a bird came flying by,
when it saw you, in horror, it soared into the sky
and hid
we drink fresh air from a bottle marked *new*
you didn't believe what they said would come true,
it did.

Listen

Everyone's talking
about something

they all know
where it's at

nobody's saying
the right thing

everyone's
sure of that.

Loaded

The hard word
spoken often in haste
is impossible to erase
it lurks behind
all future states
of mind,

an explosive device
whose timer has stopped
it may reactivate
without warning
at the slightest touch.

No Illusion

It is not an illusion
it is not what you're thinking
that ship on the horizon
IS actually sinking.

(Used in the Upstart General
Election Poster Project in 2011)

Big Bucks and Grand Crus

(i.m. Sarah)

Big bucks and grand crus
elevated style over substance.
Legendary names accused
blew the complete house down.
Record-breaking
in the wrong way
in a different league
in a world of their own.
Incredible!
A critical interruption
a big hurdle.
History will have
plenty of the stuff.
Today demands
singular talent
exceptional imagination
awesome performance.
It is not hard to see why.

The Sunshine is Someplace Else

A man on Grafton Street
holds a pole
on top of which there is a board
advertising sunglasses
in a shop that is somewhere else.
He wears a worn leather jacket,
gloves, scarf and knitted hat,
but no sunglasses.
He looks like he has come
from somewhere sunny,
he looks like he wishes he could be
somewhere sunnier than here.

The largest range of designer
sunglasses in Ireland,
it says on his board.
The sun was shining earlier
now it looks like rain again.
He pulls his hood up over his knitted hat.

A treadmill of people
moves up and down
some with smiles
some with shades
some with frowns.

A bald man walks past in a suit
he wears sunglasses and an overcoat
an umbrella in one hand
a briefcase in the other
he doesn't see the man
with the sunglasses ad
he doesn't see beyond
the papers he carries
in his tightly gripped bag.

A young man holds up a cup
he is looking for shade,
for shelter, for anything better;
a busker belts out
songs of sunshine and loss
while a couple of lovers
begin losing each other
in the depths of a slow-dance
of pain.

There's a child
in a pram, both she
and her mam have spectacles
dark on their faces;
the sellers of flowers at the corner
for hours are content that their stems
have the sunshine within
for they've come
from the sunniest of places.

The sun shines rarely now
but people still like to pretend
that it shines more often
and this, in the end,
is sometimes enough.

The sunglasses shop
is in the next street.
The sunshine is still someplace else.

Ducking but not Diving

It bores me now
all this skimming the surface
like ducks skidding across water
to pick up morsels thrown
by some passer-by
who is only interested
in a good photo shot.

And this endless search
for blame. Blame yourself
for a change.
Take your head out from between
your headlines and your deadlines
shove it under water
for a while
come back and tell me
what you find.

Here is the News

Good evening, said the newsreader
in his serious newsreader voice,
*tonight the news will be different
we are calling it "viewer's choice"*

> *so for one night only, viewers,
> we are going to let you choose
> the main headlines we will bring you
> in tonight's television news*

he tapped upon the screen of his
laptop and, voice in steady tone,
said *here are the nominations
you can text us or tweet or phone*

> *first up we have "the recession"
> when you vote call it "headline A"
> preference will be given to
> those viewers who offer to pay*

*to end this mean austerity
for the plan we deem best devised
the winner can forever say
their solution has been televised*

> *next up we have "the trouble spots"
> grouped together in "headline B"
> vote for the war you like the most
> with the outcome you want to see*

*it matters not which side you take
or how many may have to die
there are gods enough to pick from
one of them can be on your side*

our final choice is "headline C"
for which we are giving no clues
we want you to write this headline
about any subject you choose

remember that it's news we do
our programme is not like the rest
the story to make the headline
will have to depress us the best

none of your positivity
we want "nasty" in "headline Cs"
the pundits expect nothing less
the public wants value for fees

the newsreader raised both eyebrows
as he looked straight into the lens
these are the three nominations,
when I end, the voting begins.

Smoke without Fire

The doctor and the dentist
greet the scientist
they drink a toast to olden days
in their glasses
reflections of their student years
"cheers"!
No cheering crowds hail the worker
as he makes his way
through narrow streets
to meet his learned friends;
they raise another glass,
another past embraced.

The conversation takes them back
to dingy bars and dodgy
all-night party places,
to great debates on questions
scarcely understood;
the more they learned
the more they seemed to lose
but no one kept a balance sheet.

They talk of when they plotted
for the glory days to come
how everything would be different
after the revolution
how it would be for real this time
there would be a call to arms
a conscription of words
an awakening.

The voices of rebels would be heard
over those of primates and presidents
the poets and the protest singers
would write the new anthems
everything would be different.

No one saw the future creep up
becoming part of the past
they meant to change.

Now, in their pursuing way,
it is those glorious days
which raise the cheers
when comrades gather
to commemorate.

If Saint Patrick Could See Us Now

Clouded in the myths of conquests
shrouded in the mists of time
what is this State we celebrate?
This unique creation
its seeds spread wide by wind and tide
to many another nation
this island seen from a distance
adrift in the shadows
dangerously adrift
naked bruises oozing
every shift making it more difficult
to separate reality from myth.
For so long adept at being
hilariously wise after the event,
a feature of our wit,
we can only surmise at how
the future will sit.
Is there a view
or are there but images
from some death-vision?
Flashes of past deeds and dreams
subliminal scenes firmly implanted
in brains not born
in pains still torn.

What would the saintly slave make of it all,
sent to save us from eternal fall,
if he risked to walk once more among us?
Would he first set up a National Tribunal
designed to unwind our state of confusion?
The snakes he had shaken once from the land
he would find alive in the mouths of many.
Would he banish, or be banished, by a modern race
independent, yes, but still not in place?
Descendants of fairies and magical folk
would he teach us that trickery is no longer a joke?

Or, would a friend of his have a friend who works
in a place they make the piece you need
to do the deed weekends or nights
at half the price?
Would he just be redundant or eccentric and blame us
for bringing him down because he was famous?
Would he be "into Europe", maybe lead us in Brussels
or be a rebel at home with a thousand good causes?
Would he sing country and western?

> *Island of saints*
> *island of scholars*
> *send us more euro*
> *we've run out of dollars.*

Might he be a big banker
or a builder or both
or an abusive priest
playing loose with our souls?

Or, would he have the vision that could harness the power
and give unto us our yet finest hour?
Would he lead our great youth
in a crusade of truth
and revival of all that was good on the island?

Would he silence the serpents and knock from their perches
the pigeons that coo in their self-righteous breasts?

We have popped our champagne
and tasted the sparkle
but the bubbles have burst
and revealed a debacle.

So wake from your dreaming
whether soldier or saint
we are calling once more,
though our voices are faint,
we are calling in earnest
our penance is done

we are calling for someone
to once again come
to unite us in strength
with no fear of the past
to the future come lead us
to a future at last.

A Different Light

(i.m. Harry Clarke)

He saw the light in a different way
and filtered it
into tales of past and present worlds
preserved for the illumination
of future generations.

The everyday bustle shut out
by windows looking in on other lives
created from a host of saints and sinners,
a pastiche of myth and magic
displayed in deepest hues,
stylish shapes superbly crafted
by a master of his trade.

A uniquely skilled genius,
stymied and betrayed
by weak-willed post-revolutionaries
succumbing to the thumb
of dominant institutions,
exiled in search of freedom
from diseases of the day,
destined to die
without the embrace of home.

So much achieved in such short time
we can only imagine
all that was left unseen
and rejoice in what there is,
a treasured legacy
that will forever glow
with richness and grace;
a different light unfurled
around a dark and troubled world.

The Other Side of the Wall

(1991)

I wonder if they play
pitch and toss
in Leipzig or Rostock
and do they know the expression
"heads I win, tails you lose".
Like far away hills
it must seem
that beneath the graffiti
the dream
as reported
was greatly distorted.

Whatever the name or the game
however the penny may fall
it was not for this that they came
from the other side of the wall.

Guernica

With the pounding Atlantic
still sounding in my ears
I sit and listen to the local sounds
and hear waves of children's playground voices.
From an open-air café, the constant crackle
of their mothers' conversations
ebbs and flows like interference
between competing foreign stations
on an old transistor radio.
In the background, sharp and urgent whistle blasts
as the red-bereted policeman clears the way
for the rush of a local cycle race.

To my regret I understand nothing
of these spoken sounds
except the odd quick burst snatched from
occasional passing French tourists.
But whatever the dialects
such sidewalk scenes have a
universal language of their own,
local gossip
last night's television
schools reopening soon
the price of clothes and books
the choice of subjects.

It was probably much the same
the day the other noise came
unheralded by any warning whistle
business as usual
streets uncleared
children and mothers and fathers alike
barefooted, bareheaded and unprepared
an instant and innocent sacrifice.

The shock, like the cries
in the silent after-noise,
has long subsided
but it has and it will
happen again.

Breathtaking

(Genoa, 25 June, 1990)

On a hot Italian night
battalions of souls
touched
in a fountain of jubilation.
In celebration,
rediscovered inner thoughts
were uncovered
to friends
and total strangers.

In the morning
new colour patterns
in beer-stained t-shirts
reflected the mingling
of the night before
indelibly imprinted
in battered brain cells
retained for telling
in places far-flung
for generations still to come.

In the meantime
the green army
was on the road to Rome.

Trip to Canterbury

The last star fades
over Middelkerke,
the sky reddens
behind us to the east,
motorway lights before us
lay a trail
through flat Flanders fields.

Van Morrison sings
The Bright Side of the Road,
we are on the right side
heading for the coast.

I look at you
competent at the wheel,
think of all the other drives
south through daytime heat,
nighttime calm,
down pilgrim and Napoleonic ways
past temples, tombs and *terroirs*.

A seagull dives
into a poppied field,
soon we'll sail the Channel
with the lady dealing blackjack.

The white cliffs rise up,
a second dawning in one day,
on the road again
four pilgrims making progress
towards our mecca
on a Christmas stock up mission.

Tinned Fruit

He stood in the queue for a boat
at the edge of a Spanish sea
Union Jack rucksack on his shoulder

not being ones to judge by a cover
we struck up conversation
to enquire if we were in the right line

for our desired destination
yes, came the gruff and abrupt reply
that seemed to be that

as we examined the silent back
of his middle-aged balding head
he suddenly spun around

you know, you are the first
English-speakers I've met here, he said,
a mixture of relief and disbelief in his tone

the hotel is full of Spanish people
he sounded like he might invoke
some unfair trading rules

and the other thing I can't believe,
the olives they serve
are out of a bloody tin.

Overheard in Brussels

In the heart of Europe's babel tower
whiling away an hour or two
at a brasserie, with a book
and a few locally brewed beers
I overhear two men,
one of whose voices I recognise,
our *terrasse* tables separated
by a secluding hedge

one a visitor from abroad
may have had a breakdown or divorce
an affair or something worse
he comes tantalisingly close
to telling all but beats about the bush

the other had a marriage that has died
he loves his children still
but wonders if they're
suicidally bored or just ignored
when she left
she left what she did not take

now they talk of rock and roll
trying to recall a name of old
I have to stop myself from shouting out
It's Janis Joplin you are talking about!

If chance had not obscured me
from their glance I might have added
that, like one of them, I tread the boards,
he a lead, me a bit player.
I struggle still to understand
the roles we play
what meaning do they have?
Which is the more dramatic,
acting out the lives of others
or our own real life roles?

And what of those who passed before
and exited some other door
into a bar that never closes?
Are they playing still
in timeless parts
that replicate themselves
in unending repeats
or have they downed their last
paid the bill and gone
like this day's sun
leaving just the memory
of its heat behind?

Tossa Revisited

Two lovers
one scooter
the martyr Vincent
observes their kisses
from his carved out window
high above the old town square

the church clock chimes the hour
pews empty and quiet now
in the night as in the day
I walked the empty aisle
to count the steps
from door to altar

lizards dart in and out
from behind a light
half way up a wall
they pause to take stock
of the comings and goings
a drunk with a can
and a one-legged man
make their different ways home

silhouetted two floors up
my thoughts run rampant
a balcony of memories
the only sound
the pouring of another glass

all is well
in the old town
tonight.

Culture Night in Dublin

The city stretches itself
queues line up to catch an inside glimpse
of this or that building
normally closed to the outside
heaving crowds surround street activities

in Temple Bar a poet friend
hosts an open mic against the odds
of free advice from randomers
and city bureaucrats alike
all adding to the mix
of a warm Friday evening rush
of revelers and homeward-bounders
culture on the move
tune in to conversations
hear of hidden gems discovered
catch a snatch of office gossip
watch the dance of furtive lovers
listen to the bubbling babble
oozing from the mass of moving mouths

on Suffolk Street a youthful couple stroll
they eye up a footpath full of static people
in softly spoken French
they urge each other to enquire
shyly they hold out their brochure
and ask a middle-aged woman
to identify the point of interest
after a moment of confusion
the woman laughs and loudly proclaims
ah no loves, we're waitin' for a bus
the blushing couple giggle and glide away
in search of other queues

culture comes in many ways
it is often best when left unstaged.

Smile

A patch of wild flowers gleaming
in a sudden splash of sunlight –
what a difference
a smile can make
to even the most overcast
of faces.

Opening Time

That day again. Time come to make more time
to clear a way through cobwebbed-covered things
all dusty from the dark days undisturbed
to take from upper shelving down the tools
and from back walls long-handled rakes and spades,
reel cables, ladders, mowers, saws and gloves

the first day always slower than before
regaining practiced rhythm takes a while

unmissed things rediscovered under trees
a ball, an empty flowerpot, a bag
of last year's grass and soon the stride is back
the job is done and all's packed up inside

with sun still warm and chair in welcome poise
it's time to pull a cork and share a smile.

New Arrival

There lies a lily in the field
it crept beneath the moon's pale beam
to sprout fresh seeds from fertile bulb
while all the other flowers dreamt
it settled by the hazel tree
the fruit of which would ripen soon
beside the path where roses grew
near holly bushes set to bloom
with berries bright and come the day
its fragrance filled the morning air
like birdsong fills the woods with sound.

Catching Dust

Dust that flies unseen
in shaded places
is caught astride a stream
of filtered light
before it settles
into deep recesses
where no beam again
may ever shine.

I snatch a handful
of the passing particles
but for all I hold
inside my palm
so much more
is all the time
within my grasp.

There lies the difference
between sailing in the light
or resting in the dark.

Winter Sports

It was Monday
you were cooking a Sunday dinner
roast lamb and all the trimmings
I lit the fire and opened the wine.

Afterwards we played monopoly
and talked a little bit
you had all the best property
I had none of it.

We passed a pleasant hour
the log flames burned to smoulders
we locked up all the doors
put the dice back in their holders.

Later when we tossed about
in undercover dealings
I made a bid and bought you out
we pooled our inner feelings.

Snowman

The snowman sniffs the air
wishes for a snowmate
wonders why he's never seen
a snowwoman on his street.

He ponders what will happen
when the coming thaw sets in
will it be a slow, shrinking melt
limb by limb drooping off
into a slushy mush
or will it be a sudden
wake-up-in-the-morning
and there he is gone
sort of melt?
Nothing left but a bundle
splattered on the ground
a scarf, a hat
and his artificial bits
scattered all around

maybe the kids from next door
will come and roll him away
into another life
or maybe some object
from outer space
will fall and flatten him
dogs might attack him
or rabbits burrow into him
to nibble at the carrot in his face
shrivel him from the inside out

maybe there is a snowwoman
waiting all this time
in a cloak of silent whiteness
on the far side of his hedge
later they will merge
and stick-arm in stick-arm
fade into the dark.

Encounters

I might have met you once while on the road
but how was I to know you would be there?
No map to guide, no picture to compare,
so why would I have stopped or even slowed?
And yet if you had signalled me your code,
I would have shyly shuffled, unaware
that you and I could have so much to share;
I'd still to learn what nature had bestowed.
But later when we met I knew you well
although I least expected you to be
so blissful, yet so able to confound.
Instead of catching me when first I fell,
you put me in a boat that's still at sea
in search of shores which never may be found.

Beyond the Flood

You lifted up my world and spun it round,
your hands the axis for my fragile life
once tossed about on rollercoaster tides
you brought me through the waves with expert strokes
until we reached a point beyond the flood
to rest upon a calmer carousel.
Released from rushing swells we fell headlong
into a deeper pool of quietude.
We floated hand in hand like birds in flight
across the surface as our ripples spread
a signal to the shore that all was well.
You held me and refused to let me go.
I melted like a snowflake in your palm,
a teardrop wrapped inside a silken sheet.

The Night of the Swallow

She came, as swallows might, in the night
down from the mountain with heather in her hair;
she was always there at sunset and at sunrise
with the splendour of both in her tender eyes.

There's something sad about the world tonight
I understand the sky is void of light
they tell me that a man will come at dawn
saying *wake, arise, behold I am the sun*
but they cannot understand that I am the one.
When the snow comes I will start to build
a palace of ice which will be until Time's end;
it will stand a monument to my memory
depicting, as monuments do, a cold and false resemblance,
but for those who want to see they will know
that inside this iceberg there are corridors and caverns
full of all the warmth and beauty the world could need.

Water lapped upon the shore, tides of light
rose before me; with a mighty surge
I climbed the highest peak and raised a flag
flying details of my life and the love which I
had kept hidden for my lady of the Summer.
Turning away from the stage my tears began to flow.

Days later I awoke in a strange room
with a strange woman wandering around;
both of us had secrets that we did not talk about
though both of us confessed we must
live at ease and not in doubt.
But as in any revolution
the dream was clouded by continuing strife.

I turned on a light and made some coffee.
I could have walked along the canal
conjuring countless scenes in my mind

but I didn't
I went to the zoo and threw
nuts to the monkeys.
They threw them back.
I went home and made more coffee,
strong and black.

There's something sad about the way I feel tonight
it's as if I could be a master at my art
but dark clouds obscure the canvas from my sight
the paint falls to the floor like a flightless dart.

She came in the Fall but I knew her as Spring
as I walked through her fields,
soft and green in the morning dew.
She was Summer as I swam in her sky of blue.
But now I walk down stone-grey streets
with withering leaves blowing, chasing my feet
I wonder if it is time to go home
it's Winter, it's cold, it's starting to snow
soon all the streams will freeze and cease to flow.

Evening fell as I stared only to see
veils of emptiness rise from my colourless TV.
Even as the swallow flew, I too must be away.

Night Owls

The cooling heat
still sweetened
by the residue of berries
steeped in cointreau
the lingering scent of flowers
sleeping through
the few dim hours of quiet

owls in nearby woods,
said to once have stretched
as far south as Paris,
give periodic hoots
sounding half apologetic
for their disturbance

still outside
night owls in our own world
astride a garden seat
the owls in the wood
can hoot all they like
right now
we don't really give one.

Fear Flying

A lone bird flies
diagonally north-eastwards
across the evening sky
as the pink-peppered afterglow
of a hot sunset
begins to fade
and the northeast sky
is darker than
the other side
not a breeze
to disturb the full-leafed trees
the bird is flying hard
wings flapping madly
treading the air for dear life
for fear of being left adrift
in the fading light
cut loose in the dark.

Taking Stock

A mind in time
can chime like bells
      in some high-spiring church
or find in time
a rhyme that swells
      some awe-inspiring lurch
but when in time
new minds derive
      from what's already gone
new trends in time
that serve to drive
      the evolution on
come pick in time
the bunching grapes
      from off the bulging vine
and drink in time
a toast to apes
      then fizzle and decline.

Waiting

He sits, he waits, he hums a tune
the morning drags him through the day
a glimpse is caught of birds in flight
he thinks of southern skies and wine
he cries inside dry tears to ease
the knot that's tied around his soul
he seeks to find some greater hope
he hears his beating heart respond
be strong, be strong, be strong, be strong.

No More Blind Alleys

Unable to find her own way home
through darkened lanes between the light
she has hit too many walls
tripped over broken stones
no more blind alleys
the open road
will take her
all the
way.

Rumours

I could stay here forever
you said
as we lay entwined
deep in our lovers' bed
strong in each other's arms
safe and well out of harm's way
shutting out the news of tumours
and all the other
malignant rumours of the day.
I could stay here forever
you said.
I could stay
here
forever.

Waiting Room

Glimpses of familiar profiles
gliding back and forth
smiles prepared
to ward off nerves,
theirs and ours;
snatches of normal conversation
pass between stations;
a file is taken
from its place of readiness
all disappear
behind a silent door;
sudden flurries burst
from one room to another
across corridors
they carry files
heavier than the papers in them weigh

reading uninteresting articles
in obscure magazines
mindlessly watching
some programme
normally never seen
names are called
new faces take their place
to await their fates
now and then
a nod or smile escapes
when aimless gazes
happen to collide
all waiting for some reality
to replace
their unreal states of mind.

Watching the Wind

Like Summer wind she blew a gentle breeze
her presence real but not yet to the touch
she calmed the seas and warmed the night-time air
a hint of all the joy that was to come
we skipped along, she beat her quiet drum

a second wind throughout that Summer blew
unseen, unheard but all too sharply felt
with cutting edge it came to trick or treat
we chased it down the length of that dark lane
till wilted leaves began to grow again

since, sixteen seasons all have come and gone
each one a gift has borne for its own time
sweet breezes soft as kisses on her cheek
nudge us along the path to round each bend
sometimes we pause to sit and watch the wind.

Obscuring the Dark

The sun makes light
of the sea
then sets to the west
with a fiery breath
taking one more
day's light from me.

My heart holds its beat
in the sleep of the night
bringing comfort and calm
to my mind
until dawn sends the moon
off to rest for the day
and I wake to the tune
of your lips on my face.

The spark from each kiss
keeps the embers aglow
as the sun starts to dance
on the sea
each touch and embrace
fan the flames as we go
headlong deep
down into the spray.

The waves wash away
our tracks in the sand
but we make a new path
on a different shore
though we bathe in the tide
of a day that will pass
our love is the light
that obscures the dark.

Questions

What do you see
when I show you the moon
your young face wondrous
as you point to the dim-lit sky?

What do you think
as your eyes quiz mine
for just that perfect instant
before you smile
and take me off
on your next adventure?

Your outstretched arm
leads the way
your mouth makes sounds
at things we pass
whole words
half words
no words
then you laugh
one of your own little laughs
happy
but almost disdainful
as if you just made sense
of something silly
or maybe the other way around.

Shortly, you will compose
your own litany
and I will answer to your tune
but for now I long to know
all there is to see
in the pictures that you paint
on the canvas of
your eyes.

So many questions to ask.
Let us start. Let us start
soon.

Tomorrow's Words

She makes words now
words we understand
at first they were but sounds
before she understood.
We give her our words today
tomorrow she will make her own
will we still understand?
Will we be understood?

My Wife Thinks I'm
at a Poetry Reading

My wife thinks I'm at a poetry reading
the truth is I am
but I keep all my best words
all the here in my chest words
all my bare and undressed words
all the nevermindtheweather words
all the keepingustogether words
all the under my breath words
the no need to be said words
the all in my head words,
I keep them all
like the best wine
except not for the last time
but like every time is the first time.

And so for my next poem,
ah now,
that one's for later
when I get home.

Acknowledgements

Some of the poems in this collection, or versions of them, have previously appeared in: *Even The Daybreak: 35 Years of Salmon Poetry, Revival, Bare Hands Poetry, Boyne Berries Series, The Poetry Bus, Headstuff, OFi Press Literary Magazine, Wordlegs, The Runt, Census 3, Headspace, Bray Arts Journal, 10 Days in Dublin Anthology, Words & Whatnot*. Sincere thanks to the editors for including my poems in their publications.

My appreciation also to the judges in various poetry competitions in which my poems have been commended, placed, shortlisted and longlisted: Dermot Healy International Poetry Competition 2015, Doolin Writers' Weekend Poetry Competition 2015, The Red Line Poetry Competion 2015, the iYeats Poetry Competition 2014 and The Over the Edge New Writer of the Year Poetry Competition 2014. The poem 'No Illusion' was included in the Upstart Poster Project to highlight the importance of creativity in society which was run during the Irish General Election in 2011.

Additionally, I wish to acknowledge the producers and presenters of radio programmes that featured my work, including the Arena Arts Show and The Poetry Programme on RTE Radio 1, Rhyme and Reason on Dublin South FM, Liffey Sound FM and Dublin City FM

Many of the poems were workshopped in Writers Groups and Workshops in recent years, particularly in the Dalkey Writers Workshop (DWW), the Dublin Writers Forum, Workshops and Courses in the Irish Writers Centre and Workshops at Poetry Now/Mountains to the Sea Book Festival. I'm grateful to all the facilitators and participants for their feedback with a special word of appreciation to my fellow writers in the DWW.

A really heartfelt thanks to Anne Tannam, Colm Keegan and Alvy Carragher for taking the time to read my manuscript and for their valued and honest feedback as well as for their support and encouragement throughout. Thanks to Jim Lynch for his careful scrutiny of the text, to Sean Ruane who offered feedback on some individual poems and to my family for their help, advice and constant support.

To everyone who inspired, encouraged and facilitated the writing and performance of poems in this collection, including the MCs and audiences of poetry and spoken word events and festivals that have welcomed me and my work to their stages and places around Ireland and further afield, with a special nod to all who attended my solo readings, and the many members of the wider poetry and spoken word community that embraced and encouraged me in recent years, not forgetting those from a previous era, thank you all.

Lastly, but by no means least, massive thanks and appreciation to Jessie Lendennie and Siobhán Hutson at Salmon Poetry.

PHIL LYNCH lives in Dublin. He also lived in Belgium for a time. Most recently, his poems have appeared in, amongst others: *Even The Daybreak: 35 Years of Salmon Poetry, Revival, Bare Hands Anthology, Bare Hands Poetry* (online), *Boyne Berries Series, The Poetry Bus, Headstuff, OFi Press Literary Magazine* (Mexico), *Wordlegs, The Runt, Census 3, Circle Time, Headspace, Silver Apples Magazine, Bray Arts Journal*. He has also been featured on the *Arena* Arts Show and the *Poetry Programme* on RTE Radio as well as on a number of local radio programmes. In 2015, he was placed third in the Doolin Writers' Weekend Poetry Competition, shortlisted in the Red Line Poetry Competition and longlisted in the Dermot Healy International Poetry Competition. In 2014 he was a runner-up in the iYeats Poetry Competition and longlisted in the Over The Edge New Writer of the Year Competition. He is a regular reader/performer at poetry and spoken word events and festivals in Ireland and fur-ther afield, including Electric Picnic and Cúirt festivals and events in London, Paris, Brussels and New York. Phil is a co-founder of Ireland's only spoken word festival, *Lingo,* and is a member of the Dalkey Writers Workshop.